Religious Studies
FOR COMMON ENTRANCE

13+

Exam Practice Questions

Michael Wilcockson

Susan Grenfell

GALORE PARK

AN HACHETTE UK COMPANY

About the authors

Susan Grenfell has taught Religious Studies to Common Entrance and Scholarship level for eighteen years, ten of them as Head of Department at St Hugh's School, Faringdon. She is author of the textbook *Religious Studies for Common Entrance* and has led seminars on teaching RS at IAPS and ISRSA conferences.

Michael Wilcockson was brought up in Cambridge and studied Theology at Balliol College, Oxford. After completing his PGCE at Pembroke College, Cambridge he became Head of Divinity at Aldenham School and later at The Leys School, Cambridge. He was appointed Head of Divinity at Eton College in 1996 and in 2010 became the college's first Head of Philosophy. He was a Farmington Fellow at Harries Manchester College, Oxford in 2003 and Visiting Scholar at Pembroke College, Cambridge in 2010. He is Chief Examiner for A Level Religious Studies for a large examination board and Chief Setter for Common Entrance Religious Studies for ISEB. He is author of many textbooks for Common Entrance, GCSE and A Level. He is a Fellow of the Chartered Institute of Educational Assessors.

Every effort has been made to trace all copyright holders, but if any have been inadvertently overlooked the publishers will be pleased to make the necessary arrangements at the first opportunity.

Hachette UK's policy is to use papers that are natural, renewable and recyclable products and made from wood grown in sustainable forests. The logging and manufacturing processes are expected to conform to the environmental regulations of the country of origin.

Orders: please contact Bookpoint Ltd, 130 Milton Park, Abingdon, Oxon OX14 4SB.
Telephone: (44) 01235 827720. Fax: (44) 01235 400454. Email education@bookpoint.co.uk. Lines are open from 9 a.m. to 5 p.m., Monday to Saturday, with a 24-hour message answering service. Visit our website at www.galorepark.co.uk for details of other revision guides for Common Entrance, examination papers and Galore Park publications.

ISBN: 978 1 471853 39 5

© Susan Grenfell and Michael Wilcockson 2015

First published in 2015 by

Galore Park Publishing Ltd,

An Hachette UK Company

Carmelite House

50 Victoria Embankment

London EC4Y 0DZ

www.galorepark.co.uk

Impression number   10 9 8 7 6 5 4 3 2
Year   2019 2018 2017

Typeset in India
Printed in the UK

A catalogue record for this title is available from the British Library.

Contents

Introduction   iv

1   Interpreting the Old Testament   1

2   Interpreting the New Testament   13

3   Contemporary issues   28

4   Christianity   31

5   Judaism   34

6   Islam   37

7   Hinduism   40

8   Buddhism   43

9   Sikhism   46

Introduction

Religious Studies for Common Entrance 13+ Exam Practice Questions is a book of sample questions in the Common Entrance style, covering Syllabus A of the Common Entrance Religious Studies examination. The order of the chapters corresponds to the layout of the examination paper.

Chapters 1 and 2 cover the Bible texts that may be tested in Sections 1 and 2 of the examination. Each topic begins with Part a – questions on definitions related to the Bible story or particular details from the story; Part b – a summary of the Bible story; Part c – an interpretation of the Bible story and its ideas; Part d – an evaluation of the Bible story and/or contemporary ideas.

Chapters 3–9 cover the 'World Religions and Contemporary Issues' section (Section 3 of the examination).

At the end of this Introduction you will find a list of key words and their definitions – refer to this if you are having trouble writing definitions of difficult terms, such as 'justice' and 'blasphemy'.

Also available from Galore Park is a book of answers to all the questions in this book: *Religious Studies for Common Entrance 13+ Exam Practice Answers* (ISBN 978 1 471853 40 1).

→ The syllabus and your exam

If you have *not* submitted coursework you have **60 minutes** to complete the examination. You must:

- choose **one** question from **Section 1** (Interpreting the Old Testament) from a choice of four – spend no more than **22 minutes** on this question
- choose **one** question from **Section 2** (Interpreting the New Testament) from a choice of four – spend no more than **22 minutes** on this question
- choose **three** questions from **Section 3** (World Religions and Contemporary Issues) from a choice of 35 – spend no more than **5 minutes** per question in this section

If you have submitted coursework you have **40 minutes** to complete Sections 1 and 2 of the examination.

Sections 1 and 2

There are **four** questions in Section 1 and **four** questions in Section 2 and you have to answer **one** question from each section.

In each section you will find the questions are placed in **two groupings** according to the two main themes of each section. For each group of texts there are two questions. This means that when you come to revise, you can decide whether to revise one group of Bible stories or both groups for each section. Clearly, if you revise the stories from both groups then you will have a greater range of questions from which to choose. On the other hand, you may wish to concentrate on one group per section and therefore know a smaller number of texts really well but have less choice in the exam itself.

Each question has **four parts**, which become increasingly more demanding.

- **Part a** briefly tests factual knowledge or asks for a definition of a word or phrase.
- **Part b** tests factual knowledge of a biblical story.
- **Part c** tests your ability to interpret the story.
- **Part d** tests your ability to discuss and evaluate the story and often a contemporary issue raised by the text.

Section 3

There are **35** questions in Section 3. You have to answer **three** questions. Your teacher will have told you which religion or religions you have studied and therefore which questions you should attempt.

If you have submitted **coursework** to your senior school then there is no need to revise for this section.

Advice on coursework may be found in Michael Wilcockson's *Religious Studies for Common Entrance 13+ Revision Guide* (ISBN 978 1 471853371).

→ How to answer questions in this book

Use the information about the exam above to help you if you want to time yourself in preparation for your exam.

Generally, it is good practice to do the following:

- Write short sentences by using full stops frequently.
- Start a new paragraph for each new idea.
- Be aware that each question type in Sections 1 and 2 requires a different kind of answer.

Part a questions

Keep your answers to **Part a** questions very short – no more than one sentence.

For example: 'What does disciple mean?'

Your answer might be:
Disciple means being a follower or student of Jesus.

This achieves a Level 2 response as the definition fulfils the criteria: 'Gives two correct and appropriately detailed pieces of knowledge.'

Part a questions are worth **2 marks** each.

Part b questions

Part b questions ask you to tell the story in some way. Just retell the story clearly – don't be imaginative. Notice the key words used in the questions:
'**Outline**' is used when you are asked to write about a long story and there is not time to retell it in detail. Instead you should pick out the main parts. For example: 'Outline the story of Cain and Abel'.
'**Describe**' is used when detail is required and you are being asked to write about a specific part of the story.

For example: 'Describe the incident when Peter declared Jesus to be the Christ (Messiah).'

Your answer might be:
Jesus and the disciples were at Caesarea Philippi when Jesus asked them who the people thought he was. The disciples reported that some thought he was a prophet, others that he was John the Baptist and some Elijah. Then he asked them who they thought he was and Peter said he was the Christ.

This gives a good clear outline and covers the necessary detail.

The Level 6 descriptor is: 'Gives a **very good** answer: a coherent and precise description; an incisive summary of the significant details; very good command of English.'

You do not have to explain the story. Leave that for the next type of question.

Part b questions are worth **6 marks** each.

Part c questions

Part c questions ask you to explain the **background** and **theology** behind the story. This means showing that you understand what was going on at the time the story took place and what lessons can be learned from it, for example about God or about human beings. You need to make two or three points and **support** them with **evidence** from the story.

For example: 'Explain why Jesus said he had to suffer.'

Your answer might be:

Jesus said he had to suffer because he saw himself as the suffering servant described by Isaiah and not a great warrior messiah, which many Jews expected. He told the disciples that to be a true disciple means taking up one's cross. This could mean various things. It could mean being prepared to sacrifice one's own needs for the sake of others. It could also mean being prepared to die for others and for their sins. Jesus said he had to suffer as an example to his followers of the kind of life they had to live.

This answer shows that the candidate knows some background ideas about the suffering servant and is able to relate this to Jesus' discussion that follows Peter's confession. The candidate understands that Jesus' suffering was both an example of the Christian life and a sacrifice for sin.

The Level 6 descriptor is: 'Gives a **very good** answer: a coherent and comprehensive explanation of several ideas (with sound reference to background, history, other relevant passages, etc.); very good command of English.'

Part c questions are worth **6 marks** each.

Part d questions

Part d questions require a short discursive essay. They are intended to be demanding so as to sort out the very good candidates from the rest. They are designed to allow you to bring in contemporary debates about modern issues as well as to evaluate the ideas of the biblical passages.

You should argue from **more than one point of view** and then state clearly which argument is the stronger or which you agree with. Think about ways to introduce your arguments. You may like to use 'On the one hand...' and 'On the other hand...'; or you could use something like 'Some people think/say/argue...' and 'Other people think/say/argue...'

Your answers should be about three or four paragraphs long. It is important to include at least one relevant **example** in your essay. It can be from the contemporary world or from the Bible. You must include a **conclusion** that answers the question.

It might help to use this acronym to check that you have written a good answer:

TRETO
Have I shown that there are **T**wo sides to the argument?
Have I given **R**easons for the views I have explained?
Have I given at least one **E**xample to support my view?
Have I referred to the **T**eaching in the question?
Have I given my own **O**pinion and reached a conclusion?

For example: 'No one has Peter's faith and determination today.' Do you agree? Give reasons to support your answer.

Your answer might be:

Although Peter had great faith and determination there are many since that time who have shown equally great faith and strength of character.

Peter's faith was shown by the way he stood up for what he believed when put on trial. He hadn't always been like this, for example when he denied knowing Jesus at Jesus' own trial. Having faith and determination doesn't necessarily mean getting things right all the time. This is why Peter has become an important figure for Christians and the first leader of the Church.

On the other hand there are many today who have shown equal faith and determination, such as Desmond Tutu in his fight against racism and his courage in applying Christian principles of equality during times of persecution and hatred.

So, in conclusion, I disagree with the statement, even though Peter is a key figure for Christians.

This answer is about 150 words long – that is just under half a page of handwriting on examination paper.

The Level 7 descriptor states: 'Gives an **excellent** answer: excellent structure and balanced answer; very good use of language; focuses on the question; well-chosen examples to illustrate the points being made; another point of view considered, supported by very clear reasoning.'

Part d questions are worth **7 marks** each.

Section 3 questions

In Section 3 you do not need to write more than a paragraph of around 50–60 words for each answer.

→ # Key words for Sections 1 and 2

Use the following list of words to test yourself. Cover up the right hand side of the page and see how much you can remember.

Look, say, cover, write, check

Ark of the Covenant	A sacred box containing the two tablets of the Law (Ten Commandments)
atonement	Getting back into a right relationship with God
Baal	A Canaanite god
baptism	Symbolic washing away of sin
blasphemy	Speaking against God or making oneself equal to God
blessed	Given true happiness by God
Christ *or* **Messiah**	Anointed one
covenant	An agreement between God and His people
crucifixion	The Roman death penalty of being nailed to a cross
disciple	A follower or student
discrimination	Acting negatively against someone or some people
Eden	Garden in Genesis 2 where everything is perfect
Exodus	A way out or departure from Egypt
faith	Having an active trust in someone or in God
the Fall	The moment when Adam and Eve sinned and fell from grace
fasting	Going without food to enable oneself to be more aware of God
justice	Treating others fairly
miracle	An act of God that breaks the laws of physics
pacifist	Person who refuses to fight or use violent force
parable	A story or saying that compares the Kingdom of God with everyday human events
persecution	Harassment or ill-treatment on grounds of religious beliefs
Pharisee	Jewish religious teacher who taught strict obedience to the Law
prejudice	Holding an irrational view against someone or some people
prophet	A person chosen by God to speak God's message to the people
repentance	A sincere change of heart
resurrection	Rising to new life from the dead
Sabbath	The Jewish day of rest

sacrifice	Giving up something for something of greater value
salvation	Being saved and brought into a relationship with God
Sanhedrin	The Jewish ruling council
sin	Disobeying God and separating oneself from Him
Sinai/Horeb	The Mountain of God
Son of God	Jesus' unique relationship with God
Son of Man	Jesus' role as the one who would suffer for others
stewardship	Looking after the world for God
temptation	The desire to do something wrong
transfiguration	A change in a person's appearance
wisdom	The ability to distinguish between good and evil
worship	Giving praise and honour to God

1 Interpreting the Old Testament

Theme 1: God, human nature and covenant

1.1 The Creation

Read: Genesis 1: 1–2: 25

Part a questions:

1	What is the Sabbath?	(2)
2	What does stewardship mean?	(2)
3	What is the Garden of Eden?	(2)
4	What was the state of the earth before God began creation?	(2)
5	How did God create Adam in the second creation story?	(2)

Part b questions:

1	Describe God's creation of the Garden of Eden in Genesis 2.	(6)
2	Outline what God created on the first four days of creation in Genesis 1.	(6)
3	Describe how God created fish, land animals and humans in Genesis 1.	(6)
4	Outline the creation of man and woman in Genesis 2.	(6)
5	Describe the Garden of Eden.	(6)

Part c questions:

1	Explain the reasons why, according to Genesis 1, God was pleased with his creation.	(6)
2	Explain the significance of the instructions God gave humans in Genesis 1.	(6)
3	Explain what Genesis 2 teaches about the nature of God.	(6)
4	Explain what Genesis 2 teaches about human nature.	(6)
5	Explain what Genesis 1 and 2 teach about human treatment of animals.	(6)

Part d questions:

1	'Science has disproved Genesis 1.' Do you agree? Give reasons to support your answer.	(7)
2	'Good stewardship of the planet has never been as important as it is now.' Do you agree? Give reasons to support your answer.	(7)
3	'The world can never again be as perfect as it was when God made it.' Do you agree? Give reasons to support your answer.	(7)

4 'Genesis 2 is right; men and women are essentially different.' Do you agree? Give reasons to support your answer. (7)

5 'Genesis 1 and 2 were never intended to be factual but parables.' Do you agree? Give reasons to support your answer. (7)

1.2 The Garden of Eden and the Fall

Read: Genesis 3

Part a questions:

1 What is the Fall? (2)

2 What is sin? (2)

3 What is temptation? (2)

4 How did God punish the serpent? (2)

5 What is the Garden of Eden? (2)

Part b questions:

1 Describe the events leading up to Adam and Eve hiding from God in the Garden of Eden. (6)

2 Outline the part played by the serpent in Genesis 3. (6)

3 Outline the actions taken by God after Adam and Eve sinned. (6)

4 Describe the punishments given by God to man, woman and the serpent. (6)

5 Outline the story of the Fall in Genesis 3. (6)

Part c questions:

1 Explain the significance of the punishments given to the man and the woman. (6)

2 Explain what the story of the Fall teaches about human nature. (6)

3 Explain what the story of the Fall teaches about God. (6)

4 Explain why God expelled Adam and Eve from the Garden. (6)

5 Explain the significance of the Tree of Knowledge. (6)

Part d questions:

1 'The greatest evil today is racism.' Do you agree? Give reasons to support your answer. (7)

2 'Wrong-doing should always be punished.' Do you agree? Give reasons to support your answer. (7)

3 'Human nature is naturally selfish and greedy.' Do you agree? Give reasons to support your answer. (7)

4 'Everyone should always tell the truth.' Do you agree? Give reasons to support your answer. (7)

5 'It doesn't matter if one is religious or not, the story of the Fall still has a great deal to teach us.' Do you agree? Give reasons to support your answer. (7)

1.3 Cain and Abel

Read: Genesis 4: 1–16

Part a questions:

1 What is justice? (2)

2 Who were Cain and Abel? (2)

3 What is sacrifice? (2)

4 What sacrifice did Abel offer? (2)

5 What is sin? (2)

Part b questions:

1 Describe what happened after Cain brought his offering. (6)

2 Outline the events that led to Cain murdering Abel. (6)

3 Describe what happened after Cain killed Abel. (6)

4 Describe the conversations Cain had with God. (6)

5 Outline the story of Cain and Abel. (6)

Part c questions:

1 Explain what the story of Cain and Abel teaches about the nature of God. (6)

2 Explain why Cain murdered Abel. (6)

3 Explain why Cain's sacrifice was rejected by God. (6)

4 Explain what the story of Cain and Abel teaches about human nature. (6)

5 Explain what the story of Cain and Abel teaches about sin and anger. (6)

Part d questions:

1 'We are more like Cain than Abel.' Do you agree? Give reasons to support your answer. (7)

2 'People are too selfish to make sacrifices today.' Do you agree? Give reasons to support your answer. (7)

3 'Capital punishment should be given for murder.' Do you agree? Give reasons to support your answer. (7)

4 'No one ever acts with entirely pure motives.' Do you agree? Give reasons to support your answer. (7)

5 'It wasn't Cain's fault that he sinned; it was due to the Fall of Adam and Eve.' Do you agree? Give reasons to support your answer. (7)

1.4 The near sacrifice of Isaac

Read: Genesis 22: 1–19

Part a questions:

1   What is sacrifice? (2)

2   Who was Abraham? (2)

3   What is a covenant? (2)

4   What is faith? (2)

Part b questions:

1   Outline the story of the near sacrifice of Isaac. (6)

2   Describe the events that led to the near sacrifice of Isaac. (6)

3   Describe what the angel of the Lord said to Abraham. (6)

4   Outline what happened when God asked Abraham to sacrifice his son Isaac. (6)

5   Describe Abraham and Isaac's conversation on Mount Moriah. (6)

Part c questions:

1   Explain what the story of Abraham and Isaac teaches about faith. (6)

2   Explain what the story teaches about the character of Abraham. (6)

3   Explain what this story teaches about God's covenant. (6)

4   Explain what this story teaches about God. (6)

5   Explain what this story teaches about sacrifice. (6)

Part d questions:

1   'Giving things up for God is optional for Christians today.' Do you agree? Give reasons to support your answer. (7)

2   'The more you give, the more you receive.' Do you agree? Give reasons to support your answer. (7)

3   'It is always wrong to kill an innocent person; Abraham should not have listened to God's command.' Do you agree? Give reasons to support your answer. (7)

4   'One should do everything that God commands.' Do you agree? Give reasons to support your answer. (7)

5   'Abraham is a good role model for us today.' Do you agree? Give reasons to support your answer. (7)

1.5 The Exodus and Passover

Read: Exodus 12: 1–13

Part a questions:

1 Who was Moses? (2)

2 What is a covenant? (2)

3 What does salvation mean? (2)

4 What does exodus mean? (2)

5 What does sacrifice mean? (2)

Part b questions:

1 Outline what happened on the night when the Israelites escaped from Egypt. (6)

2 Describe the preparations the Israelites had to make for the Passover. (6)

3 Describe the meal the Israelites ate on the night of the Passover. (6)

4 Describe the first Passover. (6)

Part c questions:

1 Explain what the story of the Exodus teaches about God's covenant. (6)

2 Explain what was special about the food for the Passover meal. (6)

3 Explain the importance of the Passover lamb. (6)

4 Explain the significance of the bitter herbs and unleavened bread eaten at the first Passover meal. (6)

5 Explain what the Passover teaches about the nature of God. (6)

Part d questions:

1 'God should not take sides.' Do you agree? Give reasons to support your answer. (7)

2 'God always sides with the weak.' Do you agree? Give reasons to support your answer. (7)

3 'Justice is always worth fighting for.' Do you agree? Give reasons to support your answer. (7)

4 'Remembering the Passover still has significance today.' Do you agree? Give reasons to support your answer. (7)

5 'The Passover, which happened 3000 years ago, has nothing to teach us today.' Do you agree? Give reasons to support your answer. (7)

1.6 The Ten Commandments

Read: Exodus 19: 1–8 and Exodus 20: 1–17

Part a questions:

1   What is a covenant? (2)

2   What is worship? (2)

3   What is Sinai? (2)

4   What is justice? (2)

5   What is the Sabbath? (2)

Part b questions:

1   Describe two religious Commandments and two social Commandments. (6)

2   Describe how Moses received the Ten Commandments. (6)

3   Outline the first four Commandments. (6)

4   Outline the Commandments that deal with social behaviour. (6)

5   Outline the Commandments that deal with religious observance. (6)

Part c questions:

1   Explain what the Ten Commandments teach about God. (6)

2   Explain why the Ten Commandments are a covenant. (6)

3   Explain the importance of any **two** Commandments. (6)

4   Explain the importance of the last Commandment, 'do not covet'. (6)

5   Explain why keeping to the Ten Commandments will make Israel a 'holy nation'. (6)

Part d questions:

1   'The Ten Commandments could just be reduced to two: love God and love one's neighbour.' Do you agree? Give reasons to support your answer. (7)

2   'Having rules simply encourages people to break them.' Do you agree? Give reasons to support your answer. (7)

3   'Loving God is more important than loving your neighbour.' Do you agree? Give reasons to support your answer. (7)

4   'The most important right is the right to life.' Do you agree? Give reasons to support your answer. (7)

5   'Rules should never be broken.' Do you agree? Give reasons to support your answer. (7)

Theme 2: Leaders and prophets of the Old Testament

1.7 Moses

Read: Exodus 3: 1–17

Part a questions:

1   What was the burning bush? (2)

2   What is a miracle? (2)

3   What does Exodus mean? (2)

4   What is Horeb? (2)

5   What does salvation mean? (2)

Part b questions:

1   Outline the conversation Moses had with God at the burning bush. (6)

2   Describe how God called Moses to help the Israelites. (6)

3   Outline what happened after Moses saw the burning bush. (6)

4   Outline what Moses learnt about God's name at the burning bush. (6)

5   Describe what God promised Moses at the burning bush. (6)

Part c questions:

1   Explain what the story teaches about the nature of God. (6)

2   Explain the significance of the burning bush for Moses. (6)

3   Explain why God told Moses to tell the Israelites that 'I AM has sent you'. (6)

4   Explain why God's promise of a land 'flowing with milk and honey' is important. (6)

5   Explain why Moses is unsure whether to carry out God's command. (6)

Part d questions:

1   'The burning bush is the most important event in the Old Testament.'
    Do you agree? Give reasons to support your answer. (7)

2   'The real hero of the Exodus was Moses, not God.' Do you agree?
    Give reasons to support your answer. (7)

3   'It is the duty of all Christians and Jews always to help the oppressed.'
    Do you agree? Give reasons to support your answer. (7)

4   'No one can ever know who God actually is.' Do you agree? Give reasons to
    support your answer. (7)

5   'God always reveals himself in the unexpected.' Do you agree? Give reasons
    to support your answer. (7)

1.8 David and Bathsheba

Read: 2 Samuel 11: 1–17

Part a questions:

1   Who was David? (2)

2   What was the Ark of the Covenant? (2)

3   What is sin? (2)

4   What is temptation? (2)

5   Who was Uriah? (2)

Part b questions:

1   Outline the steps David took to cover up his adultery. (6)

2   Describe what happened after David saw Bathsheba from his roof. (6)

3   Describe what happened when David found out Bathsheba was pregnant. (6)

4   Describe how David got rid of Uriah. (6)

5   Outline the story of David and Bathsheba. (6)

Part c questions:

1   Explain why David's behaviour was not that of a good king. (6)

2   Explain what the story of David and Bathsheba teaches about David's character. (6)

3   Explain what the story of David and Bathsheba teaches about guilt. (6)

4   Explain how Uriah's character differed from King David's. (6)

5   Explain what this story teaches about leaders as monarchs (kings or queens). (6)

Part d questions:

1   'Those who commit murder should be executed, whoever they are.'
    Do you agree? Give reasons to support your answer. (7)

2   'Like David, people today have lost their sense of right and wrong.'
    Do you agree? Give reasons to support your answer. (7)

3   'The private lives of leaders should be just that: private.' Do you agree?
    Give reasons to support your answer. (7)

4   'Bad people make good leaders.' Do you agree? Give reasons to support
    your answer. (7)

5   'What David did was not very bad.' Do you agree? Give reasons to support
    your answer. (7)

1.9 Nathan

Read: 2 Samuel 12: 1–14

Part a questions:

1	What is a prophet?	(2)
2	What is justice?	(2)
3	What is a parable?	(2)
4	Who was Nathan?	(2)
5	Who was David?	(2)

Part b questions:

1	Outline what happened at Nathan's meeting with David.	(6)
2	Outline the parable Nathan told David.	(6)
3	Describe what the rich man did in Nathan's parable.	(6)
4	Outline the conversation Nathan has with David, after he tells him the parable.	(6)

Part c questions:

1	Explain why Nathan was courageous.	(6)
2	Explain how the parable showed David he had sinned.	(6)
3	Explain the point Nathan was making to David in his conversation with him.	(6)
4	Explain what the parable teaches about sin.	(6)
5	Explain why Nathan was an unusual prophet.	(6)

Part d questions:

1	'Making a criminal meet the person they have harmed is the best form of punishment.' Do you agree? Give reasons to support your answer.	(7)
2	'People should live and let live.' Do you agree? Give reasons to support your answer.	(7)
3	'There are still prophets like Nathan today.' Do you agree? Give reasons to support your answer.	(7)
4	'Being punished makes you a better person.' Do you agree? Give reasons to support your answer.	(7)
5	'God was weak; he should have demanded a greater punishment of David.' Do you agree? Give reasons to support your answer.	(7)

1.10 Solomon

Read: 1 Kings 3

Part a questions:

1   What is wisdom?   (2)

2   What is justice?   (2)

3   What is worship?   (2)

4   Who was Solomon?   (2)

Part b questions:

1   Outline the story of the two prostitutes and Solomon's judgement.   (6)

2   Describe the dream Solomon had at Gibeon.   (6)

3   Outline what happened when Solomon went to Gibeon.   (6)

4   Describe what happened when the two women appeared before Solomon.   (6)

5   Describe what happened one day after Solomon returned to Jerusalem.   (6)

Part c questions:

1   Explain the significance of the women in the story being prostitutes.   (6)

2   Explain what the events at Gibeon tell us about Solomon's character.   (6)

3   Explain what the story teaches about good leadership.   (6)

4   Explain in what ways Solomon was wise in his dealings with the two women. (6)

5   Explain the significance of Solomon's dream.   (6)

Part d questions:

1   'Wisdom is the most important quality a leader should have.' Do you agree?
    Give reasons to support your answer.   (7)

2   'Today people would rather be famous than wise.' Do you agree?
    Give reasons to support your answer.   (7)

3   'Having wisdom is more important than being good.' Do you agree?
    Give reasons to support your answer.   (7)

4   'A good leader puts himself first and others second.' Do you agree?
    Give reasons to support your answer.   (7)

5   'Solomon wasn't wise; he was just lucky.' Do you agree? Give reasons to
    support your answer.   (7)

1.11 Elijah

Read: 1 Kings 18: 19–46 and 1 Kings 19: 1–18

Part a questions:

1   What is a prophet?   (2)

2   Who was Baal?   (2)

3   What is Horeb?   (2)

4   What is meant by covenant?   (2)

5   Who was Jezebel?   (2)

Part b questions:

1   Outline the events that took place on Mount Carmel.   (6)

2   Outline the time when Elijah met King Ahab and challenged his prophets to
    a competition.   (6)

3   Describe what happened to Elijah on his journey to Horeb.   (6)

4   Describe what took place on Mount Horeb after Elijah had run away from
    Jezebel and hidden in a cave.   (6)

5   Describe how Elijah experienced the wind, earthquake, fire and whisper.   (6)

Part c questions:

1   Explain the preparations Elijah made in setting up his altar on Mount Carmel. (6)

2   Explain why Baal had to be challenged.   (6)

3   Explain what the events on Mount Horeb teach about God.   (6)

4   Explain what the story of Elijah's contest with the prophets of Baal teaches
    about sacrifice.   (6)

5   Explain what Elijah learns at Mount Horeb about the nature of God.   (6)

Part d questions:

1   'There is no logical proof for God's existence.' Do you agree? Give reasons to
    support your answer.   (7)

2   'Nobody cares what people believe nowadays.' Do you agree?
    Give reasons to support your answer.   (7)

3   'Violence is sometimes necessary to defend one's beliefs.' Do you agree?
    Give reasons to support your answer.   (7)

4   'Celebrities are today's false gods.' Do you agree? Give reasons to support
    your answer.   (7)

5   'We have all experienced God in our conscience.' Do you agree?
    Give reasons to support your answer.   (7)

1.12 Isaiah

Read: Isaiah 1: 10–20 and Isaiah 5: 1–7

Part a questions:

1	What is sin?	(2)
2	What is justice?	(2)
3	What is sacrifice?	(2)
4	What is discrimination?	(2)
5	What is a parable?	(2)

Part b questions:

1	Outline the sins of which Judah was guilty according to Isaiah.	(6)
2	Outline Isaiah's message against Judah's leaders.	(6)
3	Describe the ways Isaiah said Judah's leaders could turn back to God through justice.	(6)
4	Outline Isaiah's Song of the Vineyard.	(6)

Part c questions:

1	Explain why Isaiah's message is one of hope.	(6)
2	Explain why God criticises Israel's and Judah's worship.	(6)
3	Explain why Isaiah said that Israel's hands were full of blood.	(6)
4	Explain the meaning of the Song of the Vineyard.	(6)
5	Explain Isaiah's teaching on sin.	(6)

Part d questions:

1	'Isaiah's message is as relevant today as it was in his day.' Do you agree? Give reasons to support your answer.	(7)
2	'Being just and fair is more important than being religious.' Do you agree? Give reasons to support your answer.	(7)
3	'As a prophet, Isaiah should have given a more encouraging message.' Do you agree? Give reasons to support your answer.	(7)
4	'Isaiah's message is the kind that gives religion a bad name.' Do you agree? Give reasons to support your answer.	(7)
5	'Isaiah was either very bold or very foolish.' Do you agree? Give reasons to support your answer.	(7)

2 Interpreting the New Testament

Theme 1: Jesus' teaching

2.1 Zacchaeus

Read: Luke 19: 1–10

Part a questions:

1	What is meant by salvation?	(2)
2	What is repentance?	(2)
3	Who was Zacchaeus?	(2)
4	What is meant by the term 'Son of Man'?	(2)

Part b questions:

1	Describe what happened when Jesus met Zacchaeus.	(6)
2	Outline the story of Zacchaeus.	(6)
3	Describe the events leading up to Zacchaeus being a changed man.	(6)
4	Describe Jesus' meeting with Zacchaeus.	(6)

Part c questions:

1	Explain what Jesus meant when he said, 'The Son of Man has come to seek and to save the lost.'	(6)
2	Explain why Jesus went to Zacchaeus' house.	(6)
3	Explain why Zacchaeus is called a sinner.	(6)
4	Explain why the religious people must have been shocked when Jesus had a meal with Zacchaeus.	(6)
5	Explain why Jesus calls himself the Son of Man.	(6)

Part d questions:

1	'Zacchaeus is an example of a person with true faith.' Do you agree? Give reasons to support your answer.	(7)
2	'Racial discrimination is the greatest evil.' Do you agree? Give reasons for your answer.	(7)
3	'Zacchaeus did not deserve to be forgiven.' Do you agree? Give reasons to support your answer.	(7)

4   'Actions speak louder than words.' Do you agree? Give reasons to support your answer.   (7)

5   'There is no law that says we have a duty to help outcasts today.' Do you agree? Give reasons to support your answer.   (7)

2.2 The paralysed man

Read: Mark 2: 1–12

Part a questions:

1   What is sin?   (2)

2   What is a miracle?   (2)

3   What is blasphemy?   (2)

4   What is faith?   (2)

5   What does 'Son of Man' mean?   (2)

Part b questions:

1   Describe what happened once the man reached the floor of the house.   (6)

2   Describe what happened after Jesus said the paralysed man's sins were forgiven. (6)

3   Describe what happened when the four friends took the paralysed man to Jesus. (6)

4   Describe what happened when Jesus saw the paralysed man.   (6)

5   Outline the criticisms of the lawyers and Jesus' reply.   (6)

Part c questions:

1   Explain what Jesus meant when he said that 'the Son of Man has authority on earth to forgive sins.'   (6)

2   Explain what this miracle teaches about Jesus and his authority.   (6)

3   Explain why the lawyers were angry with Jesus.   (6)

4   Explain why Jesus did not think he had committed blasphemy.   (6)

5   Explain why the lawyers thought Jesus had committed blasphemy.   (6)

Part d questions:

1   'Miracles only occur in hospitals nowadays.' Do you agree? Give reasons to support your answer.   (7)

2   'Faith is as powerful as medicine.' Do you agree? Give reasons to support your answer.   (7)

3   'We should always help our friends whatever they have done.' Do you agree? Give reasons to support your answer.   (7)

4   'Helping a terminally ill person die is never acceptable.' Do you agree? Give reasons to support your answer.   (7)

5   'Jesus did not give a very good answer to the lawyers.' Do you agree? Give reasons to support your answer.   (7)

2.3 The calming of the storm

Read: Mark 4: 35–41

Part a questions:

1 What is faith? (2)

2 What is a disciple? (2)

3 What is a miracle? (2)

4 What did Jesus say to the sea? (2)

Part b questions:

1 Describe what happened after Jesus fell asleep in the boat. (6)

2 Outline the miracle of the calming of the storm. (6)

3 Describe what happened in the evening after Jesus finished teaching the people. (6)

Part c questions:

1 Explain the symbolism of the great storm and the great calm that followed. (6)

2 Explain what the story teaches about Jesus. (6)

3 Explain why Jesus rebuked the disciples for their lack of faith. (6)

4 Explain why the disciples were unsure who Jesus was. (6)

5 Explain how Jesus' reaction differed from that of his disciples. (6)

Part d questions:

1 'Science has not disproved miracles.' Do you agree? Give reasons to support your answer. (7)

2 'It is a miracle if an aeroplane crashes and nobody dies.' Do you agree? Give reasons to support your answer. (7)

3 'We need to believe that miracles happen.' Do you agree? Give reasons to support your answer. (7)

4 'Jesus' nature miracles prove that he was the Son of God.' Do you agree? Give reasons to support your answer. (7)

5 'True faith means that we should never doubt anything.' Do you agree? Give reasons to support your answer. (7)

2.4 The rich young man

Read: Mark 10: 17–31

Part a questions:

1 What is a disciple? (2)

2 Name two of the commandments the man says he has kept. (2)

3 What is salvation? (2)

| 4 | What is justice? | (2) |
| 5 | What does sacrifice mean? | (2) |

Part b questions:

1 Describe what Jesus told his disciples about wealth and the Kingdom of God. (6)

2 Outline Jesus' conversation with the rich young man. (6)

3 Describe what happened when the rich young man met Jesus. (6)

4 Describe Jesus' teaching to his disciples after the rich young man had left. (6)

5 Outline Jesus' teaching on possessing wealth. (6)

Part c questions:

1 Explain why Jesus' teaching about wealth and eternal life was surprising. (6)

2 Explain why the young man thought he had lived a good life. (6)

3 Explain what this story teaches about discipleship. (6)

4 Explain why Jesus said that it was easier for a camel to go through the eye of a needle than for a rich man to enter the Kingdom of God. (6)

5 Explain what Jesus meant when he said, 'the first will be last, and the last first.' (6)

Part d questions:

1 'Christians should give all their money away.' Do you agree? Give reasons to support your answer. (7)

2 'Helping the poor is more important than spending money on places of worship.' Do you agree? Give reasons to support your answer. (7)

3 'The love of money is the root of all evil.' Do you agree? Give reasons to support your answer. (7)

4 'All Christians should be poor.' Do you agree? Give reasons to support your answer. (7)

5 'Jesus' teaching on wealth is unrealistic.' Do you agree? Give reasons to support your answer. (7)

2.5 The woman and Simon the Pharisee

Read: Luke 7: 36–50

Part a questions:

1 What is a parable? (2)

2 What is sin? (2)

3 Who were the Pharisees? (2)

4 What is faith? (2)

5 What does salvation mean? (2)

Part b questions:

1   Describe the events leading up to when Jesus told his parable.   (6)

2   Describe what the woman did when she arrived at Simon's house.   (6)

3   Outline the parable Jesus told Simon the Pharisee.   (6)

4   Outline what happened when Jesus had supper with Simon the Pharisee.   (6)

5   Describe how Jesus criticised Simon the Pharisee.   (6)

Part c questions:

1   Explain why Simon the Pharisee was embarrassed by Jesus' parable.   (6)

2   Explain what Jesus' parable and behaviour towards the woman teach
    about forgiveness.   (6)

3   Explain what the story teaches about Jesus' attitude to outcasts.   (6)

4   Explain the parable that Jesus told Simon the Pharisee.   (6)

5   Explain what the story teaches about the woman's belief in Jesus.   (6)

Part d questions:

1   'Because Jesus welcomed all we have a duty to look after asylum seekers.'
    Do you agree? Give reasons to support your answer.   (7)

2   'People who commit small crimes should not be sent to prison; they deserve
    a second chance.' Do you agree? Give reasons to support your answer.   (7)

3   'Like Simon, we are all hypocrites.' Do you agree? Give reasons to support
    your answer.   (7)

4   'People should forgive more and criticise less.' Do you agree? Give reasons to
    support your answer.   (7)

5   'Simon was not a bad person.' Do you agree? Give reasons to support
    your answer.   (7)

2.6 The Good Samaritan

Read: Luke 10: 25–37

Part a questions:

1   What is a parable?   (2)

2   Who were the Samaritans?   (2)

3   What is discrimination?   (2)

4   What two questions does the lawyer ask Jesus?   (2)

5   What does Jesus tell the lawyer to do after the parable?   (2)

Part b questions:

1   Describe the actions of the three people who saw the man who had been
    beaten up.   (6)

2   Outline the Parable of the Good Samaritan.   (6)

3   Describe how Jesus answered the lawyer's question, 'Who is my neighbour?' (6)

4   Describe all that happened to the man who was travelling to Jericho. (6)

5   Describe the conversation that led to Jesus telling the Parable of the Good Samaritan. (6)

Part c questions:

1   Explain how the parable answered the question, 'Who is my neighbour?' (6)

2   Explain why Jesus frequently taught using parables. (6)

3   Explain the meaning of the Parable of the Good Samaritan. (6)

4   Explain why Jesus chose a Samaritan to answer the question, 'Who is my neighbour?' (6)

5   Explain what the Parable of the Good Samaritan teaches about prejudice. (6)

Part d questions:

1   'Parables are not the best way to teach about the Kingdom of God.' Do you agree? Give reasons to support your answer. (7)

2   'It is impossible to show kindness to people we do not like.' Do you agree? Give reasons to support your answer. (7)

3   'There are no really "good Samaritans" today.' Do you agree? Give reasons to support your answer. (7)

4   'It is much easier to be a "good Samaritan" today than in the past.' Do you agree? Give reasons for your answer. (7)

5   'If everyone understood the meaning of the Parable of the Good Samaritan there would be no racism today.' Do you agree? Give reasons to support your answer. (7)

2.7 The Lost Son

Read: Luke 15: 11–32

Part a questions:

1   What is a parable? (2)

2   What is repentance? (2)

3   What is salvation? (2)

4   What is sin? (2)

5   What did the younger son say to his father on his return home? (2)

Part b questions:

1   Describe the younger son's thoughts when he 'came to his senses'. (6)

2   Describe what happened in the parable after the younger son had spent all his money on wild living. (6)

3   Describe what the younger son does in the Parable of the Lost Son. (6)

4 Outline the conversation the father had with his elder son after
   the younger son had come home.   (6)

5 Outline the actions of the two sons in the Parable of the Lost Son.   (6)

Part c questions:

1 Explain what the Parable of the Lost Son teaches about human nature.   (6)

2 Explain what this parable teaches about forgiveness.   (6)

3 Explain the meaning of the elder brother's reaction.   (6)

4 Explain what the parable teaches about sin.   (6)

5 Explain what the return home of the younger son teaches about repentance. (6)

Part d questions:

1 'The father (in the parable) did not act fairly.' Do you agree? Give reasons
   to support your answer.   (7)

2 'We can behave as badly as we like, as long as we say sorry.' Do you agree?
   Give reasons to support your answer.   (7)

3 'We should always forgive, no matter what wrong someone has done.'
   Do you agree? Give reasons to support your answer.   (7)

4 'It is easier to see wrong in others than it is to see it in ourselves.'
   Do you agree? Give reasons to support your answer.   (7)

5 'The elder son was right not to have forgiven his younger brother.'
   Do you agree? Give reasons to support your answer.   (7)

2.8 The Sower

Read: Luke 8: 4–8, 11–15

Part a questions:

1 What is a parable?   (2)

2 What is persecution?   (2)

3 What does the seed represent in the Parable of the Sower?   (2)

4 What is faith?   (2)

5 What is a disciple?   (2)

Part b questions:

1 Outline the Parable of the Sower.   (6)

2 Outline Jesus' explanation of the Parable of the Sower.   (6)

3 Describe what happened to the seed when the farmer sowed his field.   (6)

4 Describe what happened to the seed that fell on rocky ground and among
   the thorns and what Jesus said these symbolised.   (6)

Part c questions:

1 Explain what the parable teaches about discipleship. (6)

2 Explain why Jesus had to explain the parable to his disciples. (6)

3 Explain the symbolism of the seeds that fell on the path and good soil. (6)

4 Explain why Jesus chose different types of soil to explain the nature of faith. (6)

5 Explain what the Parable of the Sower teaches about the Kingdom of God. (6)

Part d questions:

1 'Jesus was right; almost nobody has genuine faith in God.' Do you agree? Give reasons to support your answer. (7)

2 'The only kind of religion people want today is one that brings them good fortune.' Do you agree? Give reasons to support your answer. (7)

3 'The Kingdom of God makes unrealistic demands on people.' Do you agree? Give reasons to support your answer. (7)

4 'Everyone switches off as soon as someone mentions religion.' Do you agree? Give reasons to support your answer. (7)

5 'The Parable of the Sower is only about coping with failure.' Do you agree? Give reasons to support your answer. (7)

Theme 2: Jesus' life, death and resurrection

2.9 The birth of Jesus

Read: Matthew 1: 18–25

Part a questions:

1 Who was Joseph? (2)

2 Who was Mary? (2)

3 What is a miracle? (2)

4 What does Messiah or Christ mean? (2)

5 What is faith? (2)

Part b questions:

1 Outline the events that led to Jesus' birth. (6)

2 Outline the instructions the angel gave Joseph. (6)

3 Describe what happened after Joseph discovered Mary was expecting a baby. (6)

4 Describe the role of the angel in the story of Jesus' birth. (6)

5 Describe the role of Joseph in the story of Jesus' birth. (6)

Part c questions:

1 Explain what the story teaches about the importance of Joseph in Jesus' birth. (6)

2 Explain why the baby was called Jesus. (6)

3   Explain what the story teaches about God's relationship with humans.   (6)

4   Explain what the story teaches about the importance of Mary in Jesus' birth.   (6)

Part d questions:

1   'We have forgotten the true meaning of Christmas.' Do you agree? Give reasons to support your answer.   (7)

2   'The story of Jesus' birth tells us more about the love of God than any other.' Do you agree? Give reasons to support your answer.   (7)

3   'Children should have the same rights as adults.' Do you agree? Give reasons to support your answer.   (7)

4   'Joseph is the real hero of Jesus' birth.' Do you agree? Give reasons to support your answer.   (7)

5   'Jesus' life and teaching are more important than his birth.' Do you agree? Give reasons to support your answer.   (7)

2.10 The temptations

Read: Luke 4: 1–13

Part a questions:

1   What is temptation?   (2)

2   What is worship?   (2)

3   What is fasting?   (2)

4   What is meant by the term 'Son of God'?   (2)

5   How long did Jesus fast for?   (2)

Part b questions:

1   Describe Jesus' responses to each of the temptations.   (6)

2   Describe what happened when Jesus was taken to see all the kingdoms of the world.   (6)

3   Outline the three ways in which Jesus was tempted.   (6)

4   Describe how the devil tempted Jesus when he was hungry.   (6)

5   Describe how Jesus responded to the devil's temptations.   (6)

Part c questions:

1   Explain the importance of the temptations in Jesus' life.   (6)

2   Explain what the temptations teach about Jesus' relationship with God.   (6)

3   Explain why it was important that Jesus resisted temptation.   (6)

4   Explain why Jesus said, 'Worship the Lord your God and serve him only.'   (6)

5   Explain what Jesus meant when he said, 'Human beings cannot live on bread alone.'   (6)

Part d questions:

1 'It is tempting to use violence when presented with an unfair situation, but it is never right.' Do you agree? Give reasons to support your answer. (7)

2 'It is only bad people who are tempted.' Do you agree? Give reasons to support your answer. (7)

3 'It is always possible to resist temptation.' Do you agree? Give reasons to support your answer. (7)

4 'The end justifies the means.' Do you agree? Give reasons to support your answer. (7)

5 'Cheating is wrong even if no one finds out and no one is hurt by it.' Do you agree? Give reasons to support your answer. (7)

2.11 The call of the disciples

Read: Luke 5: 1–11

Part a questions:

1 What is a disciple? (2)

2 What is a miracle? (2)

3 Who was Simon Peter? (2)

4 What is sin? (2)

5 What is faith? (2)

Part b questions:

1 Describe the conversation between Simon Peter and Jesus after the catch of fish. (6)

2 Describe what happened when Jesus asked Simon Peter to let down his fishing nets. (6)

3 Describe what happened when Jesus called his first disciples. (6)

4 Describe how Jesus called the first disciples. (6)

5 Describe what happened after Jesus got into Simon Peter's boat. (6)

Part c questions:

1 Explain what this story teaches us about Jesus. (6)

2 Explain what Jesus meant when he said to Simon Peter, 'From now on you will fish for people.' (6)

3 Explain what the calling of the disciples teaches about being a follower of Jesus. (6)

4 Explain Simon Peter's reaction to the miracle. (6)

5 Explain what this story teaches about the demands of the Kingdom of God. (6)

Part d questions:

1 'Having faith in God means one should never doubt His existence.' Do you agree? Give reasons to support your answer. (7)

2 'It is wise to give up everything for faith.' Do you agree? Give reasons to support your answer. (7)

3 'Family comes first; the disciples were wrong to leave everything and follow Jesus.' Do you agree? Give reasons to support your answer. (7)

4 'Wealth is not a barrier to faith.' Do you agree? Give reasons to support your answer. (7)

5 'The miracle of the catch of fish did not happen; it is really a parable.' Do you agree? Give reasons to support your answer. (7)

2.12 Peter's declaration

Read: Mark 8: 27–33

Part a questions:

1 What does Messiah or Christ mean? (2)

2 Who was John the Baptist? (2)

3 Who was Peter? (2)

4 What is meant by the term 'Son of Man'? (2)

5 What is a prophet? (2)

Part b questions:

1 Outline what Jesus said after Peter declared him to be the Messiah. (6)

2 Outline the conversation Jesus had with his disciples at Caesarea Philippi. (6)

3 Outline what happened at Caesarea Philippi. (6)

4 Describe the conversation that led to Peter's declaration of faith. (6)

Part c questions:

1 Explain why Jesus described himself as the Son of Man. (6)

2 Explain why Jesus was not the kind of Messiah the Jews had been expecting. (6)

3 Explain why Jesus said to Peter, 'Get behind me Satan.' (6)

4 Explain what Peter meant when he said, 'You are the Christ (or Messiah).' (6)

5 Explain why some people thought Jesus might be Elijah or John the Baptist. (6)

Part d questions:

1 'It doesn't matter whether you believe in God as long as you lead a good life.' Do you agree? Give reasons to support your answer. (7)

2 'It doesn't matter whether Jesus was the Messiah or not.' Do you agree? Give reasons to support your answer. (7)

3   'The most important things are worth making sacrifices for.' Do you agree? Give reasons to support your answer.   (7)

4   'Jesus is important because of what he did, not because of who he was.' Do you agree? Give reasons to support your answer.   (7)

5   'Jesus was more than just a good man.' Do you agree? Give reasons to support your answer.   (7)

2.13 The Transfiguration

Read: Mark 9: 2–13

Part a questions:

1   What does transfiguration mean?   (2)

2   What is meant by the term 'Son of Man'?   (2)

3   Who was Moses?   (2)

4   Who was Elijah?   (2)

5   What does Jesus order the disciples to do on the way from the mountain?   (2)

Part b questions:

1   Describe what happened when Jesus took Peter, James and John up a high mountain.   (6)

2   Describe what happened after the vision of Moses and Elijah at the Transfiguration.   (6)

3   Outline the conversation Jesus had with his disciples on the way down the mountain after the Transfiguration.   (6)

4   Outline what happened when Jesus was transfigured.   (6)

5   Outline the story of the Transfiguration.   (6)

Part c questions:

1   Explain why Moses and Elijah appeared with Jesus.   (6)

2   Explain why Jesus told his disciples not to tell anyone about what had happened.   (6)

3   Explain what the Transfiguration teaches about Jesus.   (6)

4   Explain what the Transfiguration teaches about Jesus' mission.   (6)

5   Explain the significance of the voice from the cloud.   (6)

Part d questions:

1   'Peter can't have understood the Transfiguration if he later denied knowing Jesus.' Do you agree? Give reasons to support your answer.   (7)

2   'God can only really be experienced in peace and quietness.' Do you agree? Give reasons to support your answer.   (7)

3   'Jesus was more than just a teacher.' Do you agree? Give reasons to support your answer.   (7)

4 'God is more concerned with what we believe than what we do.' Do you agree? Give reasons to support your answer. (7)

5 'The Transfiguration is more important than the Resurrection.' Do you agree? Give reasons to support your answer. (7)

2.14 The sentence, Crucifixion and burial

Read: Mark 15: 6–47

Part a questions:

1 What was written on the notice that was placed at the top of Jesus' cross? (2)

2 What is crucifixion? (2)

3 Who was Barabbas? (2)

4 Who was Pontius Pilate? (2)

5 What was the Sanhedrin? (2)

6 What does atonement mean? (2)

7 What is the Sabbath? (2)

8 Who was Joseph of Arimathea? (2)

Part b questions:

1 Describe what happened when Jesus was taken before Pilate. (6)

2 Describe how the soldiers mocked Jesus. (6)

3 Outline the crucifixion of Jesus. (6)

4 Describe how Jesus was mocked when he was on the cross. (6)

5 Describe what happened after Jesus had died. (6)

6 Describe the role played by Joseph of Arimathea in Jesus' burial. (6)

7 Outline the events of Jesus' burial. (6)

Part c questions:

1 Explain why Jesus' crucifixion is important for Christians. (6)

2 Explain the significance of the Temple curtain tearing in two. (6)

3 Explain **two** reasons why Jesus had to die. (6)

4 Explain why Jesus was taken to Pilate. (6)

5 Explain the significance of the Roman centurion's words when Jesus died. (6)

6 Explain why Jesus' burial is important for his Resurrection. (6)

7 Explain the significance of Joseph of Arimathea in the story of Jesus' burial. (6)

8 Explain why putting a stone across Jesus' tomb was significant. (6)

Part d questions:

1 'Pilate was weak; he should not have executed Jesus.' Do you agree? Give
  reasons to support your answer. (7)

2 'True Christian love means being willing to die for others.' Do you agree?
  Give reasons to support your answer. (7)

3 'Suffering is a fact of life; people should just put up with it.' Do you agree?
  Give reasons to support your answer. (7)

4 'Capital punishment should never be used.' Do you agree? Give reasons to
  support your answer. (7)

5 'There was no reason for Jesus to die.' Do you agree? Give reasons to
  support your answer. (7)

6 'It is more likely that Jesus' body was stolen than resurrected.' Do you agree?
  Give reasons to support your answer. (7)

7 'The women at Jesus' burial showed greater faith than his male disciples.'
  Do you agree? Give reasons to support your answer. (7)

8 'The real hero of Jesus' burial is Joseph of Arimathea.' Do you agree? Give
  reasons to support your answer. (7)

9 'The story of Jesus' burial is very unimportant.' Do you agree? Give reasons
  to support your answer. (7)

2.15 The Resurrection

Read: John 20: 1–29

Part a questions:

1 What does resurrection mean? (2)

2 What is a miracle? (2)

3 What does blessed mean? (2)

4 What does Son of God mean? (2)

5 Which two disciples ran to the empty tomb? (2)

Part b questions:

1 Outline what the disciples saw when they arrived at Jesus' tomb. (6)

2 Outline the conversation between Jesus and Mary at the tomb. (6)

3 Describe what happened when the resurrected Jesus appeared to
  Mary Magdalene. (6)

4 Describe what happened when Jesus appeared to the disciples on the
  evening of his resurrection. (6)

5 Describe what happened when the resurrected Jesus appeared to Thomas. (6)

Part c questions:

1   Explain the significance of Jesus appearing first to Mary Magdalene.   (6)

2   Explain why Jesus said, 'Blessed are those who have not seen and yet have believed.'   (6)

3   Explain the importance of the empty tomb for Christians.   (6)

4   Explain why Jesus told Thomas to 'stop doubting and believe'.   (6)

5   Explain why Jesus breathed on the disciples.   (6)

Part d questions:

1   'Thomas is the most important character in the story of Jesus' resurrection.' Do you agree? Give reasons to support your answer.   (7)

2   'The only really important thing about Christianity is the Resurrection.' Do you agree? Give reasons to support your answer.   (7)

3   'Science shows that miracles like the Resurrection are entirely possible.' Do you agree? Give reasons to support your answer.   (7)

4   'There is life after death.' Do you agree? Give reasons to support your answer.   (7)

5   'It is better to doubt than to believe in something that may not be true.' Do you agree? Give reasons for your answer.   (7)

3 Contemporary issues

Contemporary issues form the first part of Section 3 in the exam.
   You can choose to answer all three of your questions from this part, or you can answer some questions from here and some from other parts of Section 3. You should check with your teacher what to do before you sit the exam.
   Remember that your answers should be between 50 and 60 words long. You should *not* give your view or opinion on the topics.

3.1 Science and religion

1   Outline what Richard Dawkins says about religion.   (6)

2   What is creationism?   (6)

3   What is intelligent design?   (6)

4   Give three reasons why many Christians think science and religion
    are compatible.   (6)

5   Outline what Stephen Hawking believes about the origins of the universe.   (6)

3.2 Stewardship and the environment

1   Outline the work of A Rocha.   (6)

2   Outline the Christian teaching on stewardship and the environment.   (6)

3   Give **three** examples of 'environmental crisis'.   (6)

4   Outline **three** moral reasons why people should protect the environment.   (6)

5   Give **three** examples of conservation.   (6)

3.3 Stewardship and animals

1   Outline **two** reasons why humans have treated animals differently from
    themselves.   (6)

2   Outline **two** Christian reasons for vegetarianism.   (6)

3   Describe the moral reasons why humans have used animals for research.   (6)

4   Explain the reasons why humans have used animals for entertainment.   (6)

5   Outline why some Christians argue for vegetarianism.   (6)

3.4 Human rights

1   What are human rights?   (6)

2   Explain what children's rights are.   (6)

3   Outline how Martin Luther King campaigned for racial equality.   (6)

4   Outline how Christian teaching supports human rights.   (6)

5   What is UNICEF?   (6)

3.5 Law and rules

1   What is the Rule of St Benedict?   (6)

2   What is moral relativism?   (6)

3   Outline **three** aims of punishment.   (6)

4   Outline the work of the Prison Reform Trust.   (6)

5   What are the arguments for capital punishment?   (6)

3.6 Leadership and wisdom

1   Explain what is meant by conscience.   (6)

2   Outline Jesus' teaching in the Sermon on the Mount on the treatment
    of enemies.   (6)

3   Explain how Dietrich Bonhoeffer showed Christian leadership.   (6)

4   Outline Christian teaching on being a good leader.   (6)

5   Give **two** different modern day examples of abuse of power.   (6)

3.7 Social justice

1   What is social justice?   (6)

2   What is Fair Trade?   (6)

3   Describe Jackie Pullinger's work in Hong Kong.   (6)

4   Outline Christian teaching on stewardship and social justice.   (6)

5   Describe how Oscar Romero worked for social justice.   (6)

3.8 Treatment of the poor

1 Outline the Christian teaching on wealth and treatment of the poor. (6)

2 Describe Mother Teresa's work among the poor in India. (6)

3 Explain why charity is central in Christianity. (6)

4 Outline what Jesus said to the rich young man. (6)

5 Outline the work of **one** Christian leader who worked for social injustice and the poor. (6)

3.9 Prejudice and discrimination

1 Outline how prejudice and discrimination lead to injustice. (6)

2 What is a multi-racial plural society? (6)

3 Outline Meg Guillebaud's work in Rwanda. (6)

4 What is the relationship between prejudice and discrimination? (6)

5 Outline **three** examples of anti-discrimination laws in the United Kingdom. (6)

3.10 Attitudes to death

1 Outline **three** reasons why some Christians consider that euthanasia is wrong. (6)

2 What do modern humanists believe about life after death? (6)

3 Outline the Christian 'sanctity of life' argument. (6)

4 Describe how Dame Cicely Saunders started the hospice movement. (6)

5 Outline the 'quality of life' argument. (6)

3.11 War and peace

1 Outline **four** conditions of the 'just war' argument. (6)

2 What is 'weak pacifism'? (6)

3 Outline why Quakers are absolute pacifists. (6)

4 Outline the reasons why Christians have different views about war. (6)

5 Outline **three** non-religious reasons for going to war. (6)

4 Christianity

Christianity forms the second part of Section 3 in the exam.

You can choose to answer all three of your questions from this part, or you can answer some questions from here and some from other parts of Section 3. You should check with your teacher what to do before you sit the exam.

Remember that your answers should be between 50 and 60 words long. You should *not* give your view or opinion on the topics.

4.1 Jesus

1	Explain three titles given to Jesus.	(6)
2	Outline the key events in the life of Jesus.	(6)
3	Outline some of the Christian beliefs about Jesus.	(6)
4	Describe what Christians believe about Jesus and God.	(6)
5	Outline Jesus' central teaching.	(6)

4.2 The Bible

1	Explain why Christians believe that the Bible is so important.	(6)
2	Outline some of the difficulties of understanding the Bible.	(6)
3	What is the Old Testament?	(6)
4	What is the New Testament?	(6)
5	What are the Gospels?	(6)

4.3 Beliefs

1	Describe some of the main Christian beliefs.	(6)
2	What do Christians mean by the Holy Trinity?	(6)
3	Describe three roles of the Holy Spirit.	(6)
4	What is the incarnation?	(6)
5	Describe what Christians believe about life after death.	(6)

4.4 Baptism

1   Describe what happens at an infant baptism.   (6)

2   Describe what happens at a typical believer's baptism.   (6)

3   Explain the symbolism of water and light at baptism.   (6)

4   Describe what happens at an Orthodox baptism ceremony.   (6)

5   Outline how baptism is the moment when a person becomes a Christian.   (6)

4.5 Prayer

1   Describe how Christians might pray.   (6)

2   Outline the different reasons why Christians pray.   (6)

3   What is the Lord's Prayer?   (6)

4   Describe the actions and symbols Christians might use in prayer.   (6)

5   Explain what is meant by prayers of: thanks, intercession and guidance.   (6)

4.6 Places of worship

1   Describe some of the characteristics of an Orthodox Christian church.   (6)

2   Describe some of the key features inside a typical church.   (6)

3   Explain the use of the pulpit, lectern and altar in a church.   (6)

4   Describe a typical Methodist or Baptist church.   (6)

5   Outline some of the features in a typical Roman Catholic church.   (6)

4.7 Holy Communion

1   Outline what happens at a typical Holy Communion service.   (6)

2   Explain why Christians celebrate Holy Communion.   (6)

3   Explain three symbols used in the service of Holy Communion.   (6)

4   Outline the different parts of a typical church communion service.   (6)

5   Outline some of the different ways churches celebrate Holy Communion.   (6)

4.8 Marriage

1 Describe what happens during a typical Christian marriage service in a church. (6)

2 Outline the meaning of the three promises the bride and groom make to each other in the Christian marriage ceremony. (6)

3 Outline the different Christian teachings about divorce. (6)

4 Outline the promises a couple make at their Christian marriage service. (6)

5 Outline three purposes of Christian marriage. (6)

4.9 Holy Week and Easter

1 Briefly outline the events Christians remember during Holy Week. (6)

2 Describe how Christians celebrate Easter Sunday. (6)

3 Describe what Christians remember on Good Friday and Easter Day. (6)

4 Explain the purpose of Holy Week for Christians. (6)

5 Outline what Christians do during Lent. (6)

4.10 Festivals

1 Describe what happens at Harvest Festival. (6)

2 Explain why Christians celebrate Pentecost. (6)

3 Describe how and why Christians celebrate Christmas. (6)

4 Outline how Christians celebrate Pentecost. (6)

5 Describe how Christians observe Advent. (6)

4.11 Pilgrimage

1 Explain why some Christians go on pilgrimage to Canterbury and Walsingham. (6)

2 Explain why Christians might go on pilgrimage to the Holy Land (Israel). (6)

3 Explain the importance of Rome as a place of Christian pilgrimage. (6)

4 Describe what Christians do on pilgrimage to the Holy Land (Israel). (6)

5 Describe what Christians do on pilgrimage to Lourdes. (6)

5 Judaism

Judaism forms the third part of Section 3 in the exam.

You can choose to answer all three of your questions from this part, or you can answer some questions from here and some from other parts of Section 3. You should check with your teacher what to do before you sit the exam.

Remember that your answers should be between 50 and 60 words long. You should *not* give your view or opinion on the topics.

5.1 Abraham and Moses

1	Describe the life of Moses.	(6)
2	Outline the key events in Abraham's life.	(6)
3	Describe how Moses and the Israelites escaped from Egypt.	(6)
4	What is the Exodus?	(6)
5	Describe the important moments of the Exodus.	(6)

5.2 Holy books

1	Describe what Jews believe about the Torah and the Talmud.	(6)
2	Outline the contents of the Tenach.	(6)
3	Explain what is meant by Written Torah and Oral Torah.	(6)
4	Outline the main contents of the Torah.	(6)
5	Describe how the Torah scroll is used in synagogue worship.	(6)

5.3 Beliefs

1	Describe what Jews believe about God and the Messiah.	(6)
2	Explain the Jewish teaching on the world to come.	(6)
3	What do Jews believe about God?	(6)
4	Outline the Jewish teaching about the Messiah.	(6)
5	Explain the importance of the Shema for Jews.	(6)

5.4 Synagogue

1	Describe the tefillin.	(6)
2	Describe the prayer shawl or tallit and how it is used in the synagogue.	(6)

3   Describe the main features of a typical synagogue.   (6)

4   Describe and explain the menorah, bimah and ark in the synagogue.   (6)

5   Describe Sabbath worship in the synagogue.   (6)

5.5 Orthodox and Reform Judaism

1   Describe the main differences and similarities of Orthodox and Reform worship. (6)

2   Describe what Orthodox Jews believe and practise.   (6)

3   Describe how and why Orthodox and Reform Jews differ in their approach to the Torah.   (6)

4   Explain why there are Orthodox and Reform Jews.   (6)

5   Describe and explain what Reform Jews believe and practise.   (6)

5.6 Family life

1   Describe the Jewish food laws (kosher).   (6)

2   Explain why the home is a special place in Jewish life.   (6)

3   Describe the duties of a mother in a Jewish family.   (6)

4   Describe the special things a Jewish man must wear for morning prayer.   (6)

5   Outline the purpose of a mezuzah in the Jewish home.   (6)

5.7 Shabbat

1   Describe how Shabbat is celebrated in a Jewish home.   (6)

2   Describe what happens on Friday evening Shabbat in a Jewish home.   (6)

3   Describe what preparations are made for Shabbat.   (6)

4   Describe what happens after the father and older boys return from synagogue on Shabbat.   (6)

5   Describe and explain the purpose of the mother lighting the candles, kiddush and blessing over hallot loaves on the Friday evening Shabbat at home.   (6)

5.8 Birth and Bar Mitzvah

1   Describe a typical Bar (or Bat) Mitzvah.   (6)

2   Explain what becoming Bar or Bat Mitzvah means.   (6)

3   Outline what happens at Berit Milah.   (6)

4   Describe the new responsibilities that are taken on by boys at Bar Mitzvah.   (6)

5   Describe the Jewish naming and circumcision (Berit Milah) ceremonies.   (6)

5.9 From marriage to death

1 Describe what happens at a typical Jewish wedding. (6)

2 Describe the purpose of the huppah, blessing over wine, ketubah and crushing glass at a Jewish marriage ceremony. (6)

3 Outline the purpose of hand-washing, visiting and kaddish when a Jewish person dies. (6)

4 Describe what happens at a Jewish funeral. (6)

5 Describe the part played by a Jewish family when an Orthodox Jew dies. (6)

5.10 Festivals

1 Describe the festival of Hanukkah. (6)

2 Describe the festival of Sukkot. (6)

3 Describe what happens at Rosh Hashanah. (6)

4 Describe the festival of the Simchat Torah. (6)

5 Outline the reasons why festivals are important in Jewish life. (6)

6 Outline how Pesach (Passover) is celebrated. (6)

7 Describe how Jews celebrate the festival of Purim. (6)

8 Describe the several purposes of the festival of Shavuot. (6)

6 Islam

Islam forms the fourth part of Section 3 in the exam.

You can choose to answer all three of your questions from this part, or you can answer some questions from here and some from other parts of Section 3. You should check with your teacher what to do before you sit the exam.

Remember that your answers should be between 50 and 60 words long. You should *not* give your view or opinion on the topics.

6.1 God

1	Describe what Muslims believe about God (Allah).	(6)
2	Explain three of Allah's names.	(6)
3	Outline the Muslim teaching on God as creator.	(6)
4	Explain why one of the most important metaphors for God is light.	(6)
5	Outline Muslim teaching about God's mercy and justice.	(6)

6.2 Muhammad

1	Outline the main events in the life of Muhammad.	(6)
2	Describe Muhammad's call.	(6)
3	Describe Muhammad's early life.	(6)
4	Outline Muhammad's message in Makkah.	(6)
5	Describe how Muhammad established Islam in Madinah (Yathrib).	(6)

6.3 Qur'an and Hadith

1	Describe how the Qur'an came to be written down.	(6)
2	Outline what the Hadith is and why it is useful for Muslims.	(6)
3	Outline what Muslims believe about the Qur'an.	(6)
4	Explain why Muslims believe the Qur'an is so important.	(6)
5	Describe how the Qur'an is used in worship.	(6)

6.4 Beliefs

| 1 | Describe Muslim beliefs about God's prophets. | (6) |
| 2 | Outline what is meant by the Five Pillars of Islam. | (6) |

3 Outline Muslim beliefs about the Day of Judgement and life after death. (6)

4 Outline Muslim teaching about the will of God. (6)

5 Describe what Muslims believe about angels. (6)

6.5 Salah

1 Explain the importance of prayer for Muslims. (6)

2 Describe the preparations a Muslim makes before praying. (6)

3 Describe how Muslims pray. (6)

4 Describe how men and women pray in Islam. (6)

5 Outline what happens at wudu (washing). (6)

6.6 Mosque

1 Describe what a muezzin does. (6)

2 Describe how Muslims prepare for worship in the mosque. (6)

3 Describe what might be seen in a typical mosque. (6)

4 Describe and explain: the mihrab, minbar, prayer hall and abstract patterns in a mosque. (6)

5 What is the adhan? (6)

6.7 Zakah

1 Outline how a Muslim performs Zakah. (6)

2 Explain the importance of Zakah for Muslims. (6)

3 Explain why Muslims give Zakah. (6)

4 Explain who benefits from Zakah. (6)

5 Describe how Zakah is given. (6)

6.8 Sawm

1 Outline the reasons why Muslims fast. (6)

2 Describe what Muslims do during Ramadan. (6)

3 Explain the importance of fasting for Muslims. (6)

4 Describe what happens during Ramadan. (6)

5 Describe times when a Muslim might be excused from fasting. (6)

6.9 Hajj

1 Describe why Muslims go on Hajj. (6)

2 Outline the main events of Hajj. (6)

3 Describe any **three** important moments of Hajj. (6)

4 Describe the places a Muslim visits on Hajj. (6)

5 Explain the importance for Muslims on Hajj of: the Ka'bah, Zamzam well, Plain of Arafat and pillars of Mina. (6)

6.10 Birth and death

1 Describe what Muslims do when someone dies. (6)

2 Describe what happens after a baby is born into a Muslim family. (6)

3 Outline what happens at a Muslim birth ceremony. (6)

4 Describe Muslim funeral customs. (6)

5 Outline what Muslims believe about death. (6)

6.11 Marriage

1 Describe a typical Muslim marriage ceremony. (6)

2 Describe what Muslims believe about marriage. (6)

3 Describe how an arranged Muslim marriage might take place. (6)

4 Explain the importance of marriage for Muslims. (6)

5 Outline Muslim teaching on marriage and divorce. (6)

6.12 Family life

1 Describe how Muslim children are expected to treat their parents. (6)

2 Describe the role of parents in a Muslim family. (6)

3 Outline the duties that parents have towards their children. (6)

4 Outline the duties children have towards their parents. (6)

5 Describe life in a typical Muslim family. (6)

6.13 Festivals

1 Describe the festival of Id-ul-Fitr at the end of Ramadan. (6)

2 Outline **two** Muslim festivals. (6)

3 Describe the festival of Id-ul-Adha. (6)

4 Outline the story of Abraham and Ishmael and its meaning for Muslims. (6)

7 Hinduism

Hinduism forms the fifth part of Section 3 in the exam.

You can choose to answer all three of your questions from this part, or you can answer some questions from here and some from other parts of Section 3. You should check with your teacher what to do before you sit the exam.

Remember that your answers should be between 50 and 60 words long. You should *not* give your view or opinion on the topics.

7.1 Holy books

1	Describe the main Hindu holy books.	(6)
2	Outline briefly the story of the Mahabharata.	(6)
3	Explain what the Vedas and Smritis are.	(6)
4	Outline what the Upanishads are.	(6)
5	Outline the story of the Bhagavad Gita.	(6)

7.2 Beliefs

1	Outline Hindu teaching on Brahman and atman.	(6)
2	Explain what is meant by atman and samsara.	(6)
3	What is dharma?	(6)
4	Explain Hindu teaching on ahimsa and the environment.	(6)
5	Explain Hindu teaching on karma.	(6)

7.3 Caste and dharma

1	Explain the Hindu teaching on caste and dharma.	(6)
2	Describe the Hindu caste system.	(6)
3	Outline the four castes in Hinduism.	(6)
4	Explain what Hindus believe about dharma.	(6)
5	Explain the relationship between karma and caste.	(6)

7.4 Goal

1   Explain the Hindu teaching about moksha (or goal in life).   (6)

2   Describe how a Hindu may reach his or her goal.   (6)

3   Describe the three paths to moksha.   (6)

4   Explain how a Hindu may become free from samsara.   (6)

5   Explain the relationship of karma, jnana and bhakti to moksha.   (6)

7.5 God

1   Describe the Hindu teaching on God and Brahman.   (6)

2   Describe **two** Hindu deities and their symbols.   (6)

3   What do Hindus believe about Shiva?   (6)

4   Outline the three paths to God.   (6)

5   Describe Vishnu and his symbols.   (6)

7.6 From birth to death

1   Describe the Hindu ceremonies when a baby is born.   (6)

2   Describe the Hindu sacred thread ceremony.   (6)

3   Describe what happens at a typical Hindu wedding.   (6)

4   Outline Hindu teaching about death.   (6)

5   Describe a typical Hindu funeral.   (6)

7.7 Pilgrimage

1   Explain the importance of pilgrimage for Hindus.   (6)

2   Describe a place a Hindu might go to on pilgrimage.   (6)

3   Explain why pilgrimage is a time of spiritual cleansing for Hindus.   (6)

4   Describe why Varanasi is an important pilgrimage site for Hindu pilgrims.   (6)

5   Explain why Hindus make pilgrimages to the Ganges.   (6)

7.8 Festivals

1   Outline any **two** Hindu festivals.   (6)

2   Describe the festival of Dassehra.   (6)

3   Describe what happens during the festival of Divali.   (6)

4   Outline what happens during the festivals of Holi and New Year.   (6)

5   Explain why festivals are important in Hinduism.   (6)

7.9 Worship at home

1   Describe how a shrine is made and looked after in the home.   (6)

2   Outline how Hindus prepare themselves for worship.   (6)

3   What happens at puja in the Hindu home?   (6)

4   Explain the importance of the murti in puja at home.   (6)

5   Explain the use of the lamp, murti, flowers, prashad and mantras when worshipping at the shrine in the home.   (6)

7.10 Temple

1   Describe a typical Hindu temple.   (6)

2   Describe the duties of a priest in a Hindu temple.   (6)

3   In a Hindu temple briefly explain the significance of the: spire, carvings, vihara and shrine (shikara).   (6)

4   Outline puja in the temple.   (6)

5   What is the arti ceremony in the temple?   (6)

8 Buddhism

Buddhism forms the sixth part of Section 3 in the exam.

You can choose to answer all three of your questions from this part, or you can answer some questions from here and some from other parts of Section 3. You should check with your teacher what to do before you sit the exam.

Remember that your answers should be between 50 and 60 words long. You should *not* give your view or opinion on the topics.

8.1 Siddhartha

1   Describe Siddhartha's life before his quest.   (6)

2   Explain why Siddhartha's father tried to protect him from knowledge of suffering and death.   (6)

3   How did Siddhartha's father try to protect him from knowledge of suffering and death?   (6)

4   Outline the main events in Siddhartha's early life.   (6)

5   Explain why Siddhartha was not completely happy with his life in his father's palace.   (6)

8.2 Siddhartha's quest

1   Describe Siddhartha's (the Buddha)'s quest.   (6)

2   Outline the main events of Siddhartha's quest.   (6)

3   Describe the four sights that led Siddhartha to begin his quest.   (6)

4   Describe Siddhartha's life as an ascetic (someone who chooses to live by strict disciplines).   (6)

5   Explain why Siddhartha began his quest.   (6)

8.3 The Enlightened One

1   Describe the moment when the Buddha achieved enlightenment.   (6)

2   Describe what happened when Siddhartha sat under the Bodhi tree.   (6)

3   Describe Siddhartha's temptations as he sat under the Bodhi tree.   (6)

4   Outline the events leading up to Siddhartha's moment of enlightenment.   (6)

5   Describe the moment Siddhartha became the Buddha (Enlightened One).   (6)

8.4 The Dharma

1 Explain the Buddhist teaching on karma.   (6)

2 Describe the Four Noble Truths.   (6)

3 Outline the Three Universal Truths.   (6)

4 Outline the Noble Eightfold Path.   (6)

5 Explain the Buddhist teaching on nirvana.   (6)

8.5 Sangha

1 Explain the Buddhist teaching about the sangha (community).   (6)

2 What are the roles of monks (bhikkhus) and nuns (bhikkhunis) in
   the sangha?   (6)

3 Why is the sangha important for Buddhists?   (6)

4 Outline how belonging to the sangha helps a Buddhist lead a good life.   (6)

5 Describe how the sangha was formed and developed.   (6)

8.6 Types of Buddhism

1 Describe the main characteristics of Mahayana Buddhism.   (6)

2 What is Western Buddhism?   (6)

3 What is Pure Land Buddhism?   (6)

4 What is Zen Buddhism?   (6)

5 Briefly outline Theravada and Tibetan Buddhism.   (6)

8.7 Refuge

1 Describe what it means to 'go for refuge' in the Buddha.   (6)

2 Outline the three refuges.   (6)

3 Outline what a Buddhist should do when he or she 'goes for refuge'.   (6)

4 Describe and explain the symbolism of the offerings made when a person
   goes for refuge at a shrine.   (6)

5 Describe how someone can become a Buddhist.   (6)

8.8 Buddha images

1 Describe some of the different Buddha images.   (6)

2 Describe the ways Buddhist images influence a person's life.   (6)

3 Explain the following Buddhist symbols: flame from the Buddha's head;
   image of stepping down; thunderbolt.   (6)

4   What is a bodhisattva?   (6)

5   Describe how Buddha images can be used in meditation.   (6)

8.9 Shrines, temples and monuments

1   Describe Buddhist worship (puja) at a shrine.   (6)

2   Explain **two** important Buddhist symbols or images at a shrine.   (6)

3   Describe typical worship (puja) at a Buddhist temple.   (6)

4   Explain the purpose of stupas for Buddhist pilgrims.   (6)

5   Describe a typical Buddhist shrine.   (6)

8.10 Festivals

1   Outline the Buddhist teaching on festivals.   (6)

2   Describe the festival of Pavarana Day and Kathina.   (6)

3   Outline what happens at the Buddhist festival of Wesak.   (6)

4   Describe what happens at Nirvana Day.   (6)

5   Explain the purpose of offerings at Buddhist festivals.   (6)

8.11 Buddhist way of life

1   Outline the Buddhist teaching on the environment.   (6)

2   Outline the Buddhist Five Precepts.   (6)

3   Describe and explain any **three** of the Five Precepts.   (6)

4   Explain why many Buddhists are vegetarians.   (6)

5   Why should Buddhists avoid damaging the earth?   (6)

8.12 Scriptures

1   What are the Buddhist scriptures?   (6)

2   Describe how the Tripitaka is made up.   (6)

3   Explain how a Buddhist might use the scriptures in his or her life.   (6)

4   What is a koan?   (6)

5   What are the Jataka Tales?   (6)

9 Sikhism

Sikhism forms the seventh part of Section 3 in the exam.

You can choose to answer all three of your questions from this part, or you can answer some questions from here and some from other parts of Section 3. You should check with your teacher what to do before you sit the exam.

Remember that your answers should be between 50 and 60 words long. You should *not* give your view or opinion on the topics.

9.1 Guru Nanak

1	Outline the life of Guru Nanak.	(6)
2	Describe the things that showed Guru Nanak to be a great religious teacher.	(6)
3	Describe Guru Nanak's life after his experience by the river.	(6)
4	Describe how Guru Nanak spread his teaching.	(6)
5	Describe how Guru Nanak chose his successor.	(6)

9.2 Guru Angad and Guru Gobind Rai

1	Outline the life of Guru Angad.	(6)
2	Outline the life of Guru Gobind Rai.	(6)
3	Describe how Guru Gobind Rai selected his 'five beloved ones' at Vaisakhi.	(6)
4	Describe how Guru Gobind Rai's new community, the Khalsa, began.	(6)
5	Explain how Gobind Rai made the Sikhs strong.	(6)

9.3 The Khalsa

1	What is the Khalsa?	(6)
2	Describe the five Ks.	(6)
3	Explain why members of the Khalsa take the name Singh or Kaur.	(6)
4	Describe and explain: kangha, kachha and kirpan.	(6)
5	Explain why the wearing of the five Ks is important for members of the Khalsa.	(6)

9.4 Guru Granth Sahib

| 1 | Describe how Sikhs show respect for the Guru Granth Sahib. | (6) |
| 2 | Outline the contents of the Guru Granth Sahib. | (6) |

3   Describe how Sikhs use the Guru Granth Sahib.   (6)

4   Explain how the Guru Granth Sahib is important for Sikhs.   (6)

5   Describe how the Guru Granth Sahib came to be written.   (6)

9.5 Rahit Maryada

1   Outline Sikh teaching on right conduct (the Rahit).   (6)

2   Outline the Rahit's teaching on Sikh family life.   (6)

3   Outline how and why the Rahit came to be written.   (6)

4   Describe how Sikhs should behave towards others.   (6)

5   Outline the Rahit's teaching on Sikh life in the community.   (6)

9.6 Beliefs

1   Explain the Sikh teaching about reincarnation and the goal of life.   (6)

2   Outline the Sikh teaching about God in the Mul Mantra.   (6)

3   Explain the Sikh teaching on reincarnation.   (6)

4   What is mukti and how is it achieved?   (6)

5   What is the Sikh teaching on the gurus?   (6)

9.7 Birth and initiation

1   Describe how a new baby is received into the Sikh community.   (6)

2   Describe the ceremony that takes place when a baby is born.   (6)

3   Describe how a name is given to a newborn child.   (6)

4   Describe how a person is initiated fully into Sikhism.   (6)

5   Outline what takes place at the Amritsanskar (initiation) ceremony.   (6)

9.8 The gurdwara

1   Describe worship (diwan) in the gurdwara.   (6)

2   Explain the importance of the langar (free kitchen).   (6)

3   Describe what can be seen in a typical gurdwara.   (6)

4   Describe the following in the gurdwara: the Nishan Sahib, diwan, palki,
    takht and manji.   (6)

5   Describe and explain kirtan, meditation, Karah Parshad and japji in
    Sikh worship.   (6)

9.9 Festivals

1 Outline **two** Sikh festivals. (6)

2 Describe the part played by the Guru Granth Sahib in Sikh festivals. (6)

3 Describe how the Nishan Sahib (flag) is used in festivals. (6)

4 Describe how Sikhs celebrate Vaisakhi. (6)

5 Describe how Sikhs celebrate Diwali. (6)

9.10 Marriage and death

1 Describe a typical Sikh wedding. (6)

2 Describe what happens at a Sikh funeral. (6)

3 Outline Sikh teaching on marriage. (6)

4 Outline Sikh teaching on death. (6)

5 What ceremonies take place before and after someone dies? (6)

9.11 Places of pilgrimage

1 Outline what is meant by the Five Takhts. (6)

2 Describe the Golden Temple at Amritsar. (6)

3 Outline the religious features of the Golden Temple at Amritsar. (6)

4 Describe the layout of the Golden Temple at Amritsar. (6)

5 Describe what worshippers must do when they visit the Golden Temple at Amritsar. (6)